MW00427153

Dedicated to our family: Emily Gil, Michael Gil, Vivian Gil, Lil Luis Berros, Alexandra Berros, Martha Berros, and all of Mr. Gil's students throughout the years. Especially, Claude Pepper Elementary School's 2003 second grade class.

Swim, swim, swim...

Good evening Kiddos!!
This is Willy The Walrus with breaking news from the
Bering Sea. Due to overfishing in the Alaskan coast,
there has been a lack of fish for killer whales to eat.
These enormous creatures have had no alternative or
choice, but to hunt otters and seals. The following is
a true story about a brave little otter and his
encounter with a ferocious killer whale. We wish you
luck, Billy. Take it away!

There once was an otter named Billy,
who had a fur coat and was silly.
His coat kept him from getting chilly.
Oh, Little Billy!

One day he saw a big tail of a
killer whale named Punch.

But Billy knew that if he hung around,
he'd turn into Punch's lunch.

Swim, swim, swim little Billy!
Find a safe spot that's shallow.

Since orcas live in the deep blue sea,
the kelp is the place to be.

One day Billy was munchin'.
Munchin' on a plump sea urchin.

But in the deep sea,
Punch was waiting
for little Billy.

Suddenly, Billy had drifted off to sea and there was Punch behind him.

But Billy sensed that there was something wrong...

So he

Zigged

and

Zagged,

and swam really
fast.
And left the
bully all alone!

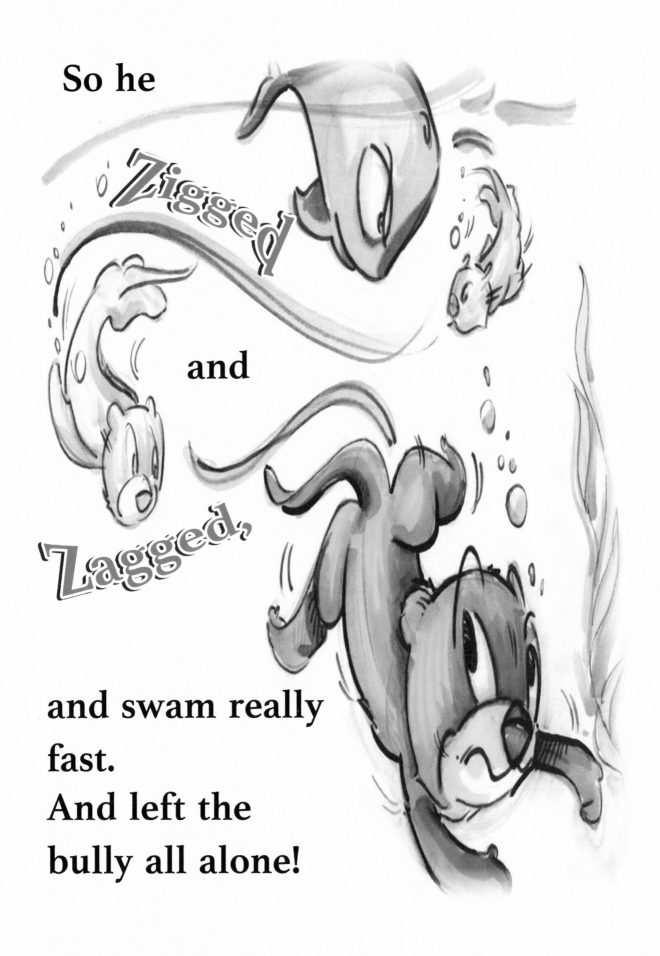

But it wasn't long, 'til Punch caught up.

So, Billy had to rev it up.

So swim, swim, swim little Billy.
Find a safe spot that's shallow.

Since orcas live in the deep
blue sea,
the kelp is the place to be.

So swim, swim, swim little Billy.
Find a safe spot that's shallow.

Since orcas live in the deep blue sea,
the kelp is the place to be.

Yeah! Yeah! The kelp is the place to be.
Yeah! Yeah! The kelp is the place to be.

Like my daughter Emily says, QUE?

alternative- choice

kelp forest- high density large sea grass which grows
in polar coastal oceans; It usually grows in shallow waters

killer whales - called orcas, they are the largest in the dolphin family **Fun Facts**: Killer whales prey mostly on fish, but they have been   known to
eat otters, seals, and dolphins. Killer whales are APEX predators. This means
that they do not have predators preying on them.

sea otter- a marine mammal that lives in the upper North Pacific Ocean
Fun Fact: Sea otters are part of the weasel family. Sea otters' fur is the
thickest in the animal kingdom. For this reason, sea otters do not feel cold
even in the most lowest temperatures.

sea urchins - a marine animal that has a flattern shell covered in spines
measuring between 3cm to 10cm
Fun Fact: They reside in shallow water, up to 5000 meters deep. They are
always eating kelp.

shallow- water that is not deep

Download the song Billy The Otter on iTunes.
Follow us on Facebook at www.facebook.com/billytheotter
and on www.billytheotter.com. Thank you!!!

Here is the article that inspired the song and brought Billy The Otter to life.
http://www1.ucsc.edu/oncampus/currents/98-99/10-19/killer.htm

86684955R00015

Made in the USA
Columbia, SC
15 January 2018